Contents

Words that appear in **bold** can be found in the glossary on pages 28–29.

What are mountains?

Mountains are areas of high, rocky land. The tallest mountain **peaks** reach up above the clouds, where it is too cold for animals and plants to live and grow.

Mountain ranges

Groups of mountains are called mountain ranges. The highest range with the tallest mountains is the Himalayas in Asia. The Andes is the longest and second highest mountain range in the world. It stretches along the west coast of South America and runs through seven countries.

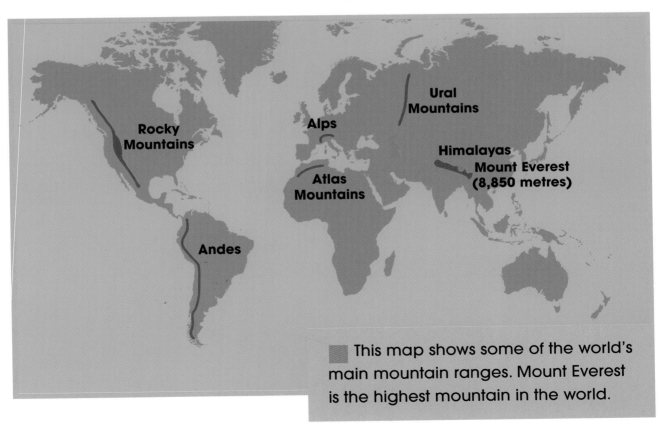

Ural Mountains

Rocky Mountains

Alps

Himalayas
Mount Everest
(8,850 metres)

Atlas Mountains

Andes

This map shows some of the world's main mountain ranges. Mount Everest is the highest mountain in the world.

The Ural Mountains in Russia are 200 million years old. They have a flat, blunt shape.

Young and old

Mountains were formed at different times in the Earth's history. You can sometimes tell which mountains are younger and which are older by their shape. The youngest mountains are the most pointed and jagged. The peaks and sharp edges of the oldest mountains have been worn away over time.

Mauna Kea is called the 'white mountain' because its peak is covered with snow in winter.

Underwater mountains

We can't see some of the greatest mountains on Earth because they lie beneath the oceans. Mauna Kea in Hawaii is nearly 9,449 metres high from the seabed, taller than Mount Everest on land. But we can only see about a third of it. The lower slopes of Mauna Kea lie beneath the ocean water.

Mountain types

The Earth's **crust** is made up of huge plates that fit together like a giant jigsaw. Mountains are formed over millions of years by the slow movement of these plates.

Fold and block mountains

The place where two plates meet is called a fault. When two plates crash together, layers of soft rock are pushed upwards and form **fold mountains**. Sometimes when the plates move, layers of hard rock between them are pushed upwards to form **block mountains**. If the rocks fall downwards between the plates, they form a valley with block mountains on either side.

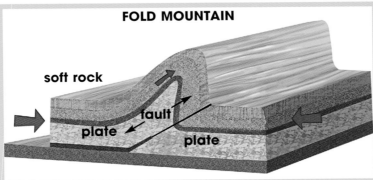

FOLD MOUNTAIN

soft rock

fault

plate

plate

■ Fold mountains form when soft rocks are pushed together. The Himalayas grow about six centimetres a year because the plates that formed them keep colliding.

■ Block mountains, such as the Sierra Nevada Mountains in the USA, form when the Earth's plates move and force blocks of hard rock up or down.

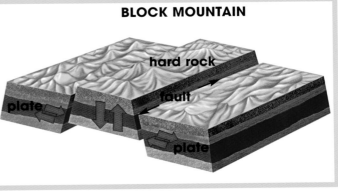

BLOCK MOUNTAIN

hard rock

fault

plate

plate

Mountain shapes

The shape of a mountain is wide around the bottom, with sloping sides rising up to a pointed peak at the top. All mountains have the same basic shape. Block mountains have slightly flatter peaks than fold mountains.

The pointed shape of K2 in the Himalayas stands out against the sky.

Make a model mountain

You will need:
- card • scissors • masking tape • large sheet of thick cardboard • newspaper
- bowl and spoon • water
- flour • salt • scales • paints
- dark green tissue paper
- glue • tin foil

1 Make a card cone using a semi-circle of card. Tape it together and stand it on the sheet of cardboard.

2 Make some scrunched-up newspaper shapes and tape them to the cone to give your mountain a rugged shape.

3 In a bowl, mix 375 ml of water, 75 grams of flour and 7 grams of salt to make a smooth glue paste.

4 Tear strips of newspaper about 6 cm by 3 cm. Dip them into the glue paste and use them to cover the cone. Leave to dry.

5 Paint white snow at the peak, grey rock below and green pasture below the rock. Stick on small tissue paper trees. Add thin ribbons of foil for mountain streams.

9

Erosion

The shape and size of mountains is constantly changed by **erosion**. A kind of erosion called **weathering** takes place when wind, rain and ice break up rock and wear the mountain away.

Glaciers

Rivers of ice, called **glaciers**, are formed high up a mountain where the weather is very cold. They move downhill very slowly. Rocks and soil trapped in the heavy ice grind away the mountainside and carve out U-shaped valleys.

Glaciers form when layers of snow build up over many years.

These people are using sticks to help them walk over a scree slope.

Scree

Loose rocks are pulled down the mountainside by the force of **gravity**. They break off more rock and soil as they fall. **Scree**, made up of fallen bits of rock and small stones, collects at the bottom of mountain slopes in heaps. Scree is difficult and dangerous to walk over.

Make a mountain erode

Ask an adult to help you with this activity

You will need:
- sharp pencil • large aluminium foil tray (e.g. a roasting tray) • rocks • small stones • gravel • sand
- soil • water • rubber gloves
- watering can with spray end attached

1 Ask an adult to help you use a sharp pencil to pierce the sides of the foil tray with several holes. Place it on flat ground outside.

2 Build a mountain in the tray. Make a mountain shape with rocks. Add small stones to complete the shape. Mix the gravel,

sand and soil with a little water to make a thick paste. Wearing rubber gloves, pat the mixture into the mountain shape to hold it together.

3 Use the watering can to sprinkle water onto the mountain top and watch the mountain gradually erode.

The water washes away the soft sand and soil, while the hard rocks and stones are left behind. Some stones tumble down the mountainside.

Volcanoes

Some mountains are **volcanoes**. They form when **molten rock**, called magma, **erupts** and bursts through faults in the Earth's crust. **Lava** pours down the sides of the volcano. It cools and hardens, changing the shape of the mountain.

Active volcanoes

An active volcano erupts regularly, sending lava, hot ash and gas into the air. A sleeping (or dormant) volcano may not have erupted for thousands of years, but it could erupt at any time! An **extinct** volcano will never erupt again.

An active volcano erupted on the island of Montserrat in 1997.

These volcanoes in Indonesia are part of the 'ring of fire'.

Ring of fire

There are about 850 active volcanoes in the world. Most active volcanoes are in what is called the 'ring of fire' around the edges of the Pacific Ocean, where moving plates weaken the Earth's crust and let magma through.

Make an open-out erupting volcano

You will need:
- sheet of A3 card • pencil
- paints • PVA glue • glitter
- grey tissue paper
- marker pens

1 With the long edges of the card at the top and bottom, fold the short edges of the card inwards to meet in the middle. Press down firmly on the folds.

2 Draw a volcano shape on the closed flaps, with a **crater** one third of the way down from the top of the paper. Paint the volcano to show rocky slopes with grass and trees at the bottom. Leave to dry.

3 Open out the flaps and copy the volcano in the picture below on to the middle section. Paint this volcano erupting. Mix red and orange paint with PVA glue and glitter for the lava. Use tissue paper for the smoke and ash.

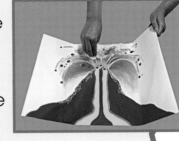

4 Label the parts of the volcano – *crater, lava, smoke, ash, gas, vent, magma*. Use books or the Internet to help you. Open and close the flaps to show your volcano erupting.

crater

Can you add the other five labels?

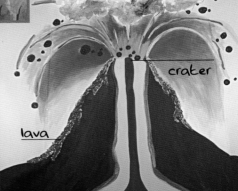

crater

lava

13

Mountain weather

It is very cold at the top of mountains. In high places the air is thin because as air rises, it spreads out. This high, thin air holds less heat from the Sun than air lower down.

Avalanche!

When the winter snow high up a mountain begins to melt in the spring, there is danger of an **avalanche**. This is when snow and ice crashes down a mountainside.

This huge avalanche will cover nearby houses with snow and ice.

These walkers are carrying extra clothes for colder weather.

Changeable weather

Mountain weather changes very quickly. A day that starts fine and dry can quickly change to wind, rain and snow. Weather at the bottom of a mountain is often quite different from the weather at the **summit**. Walkers must pack the right equipment for a day in the mountains.

Plan a day out in the mountains

1 Use the Internet to find out the weather on a particular mountain.

weather forecast

| Home | Weather News | Travel | Photo Gallery | Full Coverage | Site Map |

Weather
A relatively cloudy start with a few showers, falling as snow over summits. However, the day should become brighter and mostly dry with some sunny intervals developing.

Visibility
Mostly good but moderate in early showers. Hill fog possible above 200 metres.

Wind and temperature at 900 metres
Northerly 24 to 32 km/h. Variable 16 km/h later. Around 1°C.

Freezing level
Mostly just above summits.

Hazards
Hill fog.

2 Use this information to make a list of all the things you would need for a walk in the mountains that day. What kind of bag would you use to carry your belongings? What items would you take to keep safe in the mountains?

15

Mountain zones

The changing nature of the air as you go up a mountain creates different areas called zones. Each zone has different weather that affects the scenery, plants and animals.

Mountain top

At the top of a mountain, there is only snow, ice and bare rock. A little lower, in the upper zone, it is too cold for plants, animals and people to live there. Strong winds whip up **blizzards**. Water is permanently frozen and glaciers are formed.

At the top of this mountain, it is cold and windy above the clouds.

This house has a sloping roof so the snow slides off in winter.

Middle and lower zones

In winter, the middle and lower zones can be covered in snow. But in spring and summer, the snow melts. The melted snow forms streams that run downhill into rivers. The middle and lower zones are warm enough for plants, animals and people to live there.

16

Design a mountain home

You will need:
- sheet of A3 card • sheet of A5 card • pencil • scissors
- glue • pens or paints

1 You want to build a new home in the mountains. Think of all the things you need to consider:

a) Where will you build your home?

b) How will you decorate it – to stand out or to blend in with the surroundings?

c) How will you make it suitable for the weather?

d) Are there local **materials** you could use to build it?

2 Find a photograph of a mountain from a magazine or from the Internet. Draw the mountain on your large sheet of card and label the four zones. Colour or paint your mountain scene.

3 Design and draw your mountain home on the sheet of A5 card. Colour and cut it out. Choose a mountain zone where you would like to live. Stick your new home in place and label the different features.

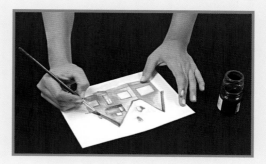

4 Ask a friend to design a mountain home. Have you chosen to live in similar zones? Discuss your reasons for your home design and location.

zone 1

Sloping roof for snow and rain

zone 2

Big windows and balcony for the view!

zone 3

Local wood for the walls and roof

zone 4

Mountain plants

If you climb a mountain, you will see different plants growing on the slopes as you go higher and higher and the air becomes thinner and colder.

Trees

Broad-leaf trees, such as beech and oak, grow on the lower slopes. **Coniferous trees**, such as pine and spruce, grow on the steeper slopes above. Their leaves are thin, tough needles and their trunks have thick bark to protect them from the strong winds.

Heavy snow slides off the sloping branches of these pine trees.

Flowers

Mountain plants have strong roots, short stems and small flowers that grow close to the ground for protection from icy winds. They flower for a short time in the spring.

Mountain flowers put on a colourful display to attract insects in spring.

18

Make a miniature rock garden

Make this miniature garden to watch real mountain plants grow!

You will need:
- seed tray • flat tray • soil
- sand • rocks • alpine plants (from a garden centre)
- gravel • empty cleaning spray bottle • water

1 Put the seed tray on the flat tray (to catch waste water).

2 Mix the sand and soil. Add a layer of the mixture to the seed tray. Arrange your rocks on top of the layer and fill the gaps with more sand and soil.

3 Make holes in the soil for your alpine plants. Place the roots of a plant in the hole, add more soil and press it around the plant carefully. Repeat with the other plants. Sprinkle a layer of gravel over the rest of the soil. Spray with water.

4 Place your tray by a window in a cool, light position. Don't let the plants dry out.

Here are some alpine plants. You can find more at a garden centre.

pink moss

candytuft

gentian

Mountain animals

Mountain animals have learned to survive by adapting to the harsh weather and the rugged, rocky slopes of their mountain homes.

Birds and insects

High up the mountain, it is very windy. Only big birds with powerful wings can fly there. Spiders and insects without wings can live higher up the mountain than any other animal.

A condor uses its large wings to soar between high mountain peaks.

This mountain hare is almost invisible against the white snow.

Mammals

Mountain **mammals** have thick, warm coats to protect them from the cold. Nimble deer and goats have hooves that spread out to grip the ground as they leap from rock to rock. Some animals have white fur, which makes it difficult for other animals to see them in the snow. They are **camouflaged**.

Play a mountain zone game

You will need:
- A3 paper • pencil and pens
- card • scissors

1 Draw a mountain on the paper and divide it into four zones – Zone 1 at the top, Zone 4 at the base. Colour your mountain.

2 Cut the card into 16 playing card-sized rectangles – four for each zone. Draw a picture on each card, with a label. Use the table below as guide.

3 Spread out the cards face down on the floor or a table.

4 With three friends, each choose a mountain zone.

Turn over a card. If the card describes your zone, lie it on the mountain in the correct place. If not, turn the card back over and the next person has a go. Try to remember where the cards you need are. The first with all four cards for their mountain zone is the winner!

	Weather	Feature	Plant	Animal
Zone 1	blizzard	bare rock	no plants	condor
Zone 2	snow and ice	glacier	moss	spider
Zone 3	spring thaw	mountain stream	alpine flower	mountain goat
Zone 4	warm summer	gentle slope	pine trees	reindeer

Living in the mountains

High up in the mountains, people live among beautiful scenery. The air is clean and mountain water is fresh. People have grown used to walking long distances along trails too narrow and rocky for cars or trucks.

Farming

On the lower mountain slopes, the rich soil is good for farming. On the steep slopes above, farmers cut **terraces** in the mountainside to make fields for their crops, such as corn and rice. Mountain sheep, goats, llamas and yaks provide milk and meat to eat.

These terraces make steep mountain slopes suitable for farming.

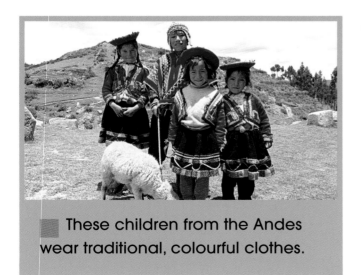
These children from the Andes wear traditional, colourful clothes.

Traditional way of life

Mountain people have often been cut off from the rest of the world. They are proud of their own languages and way of life. Today, it is easier for people to visit the mountains, so the old ways are starting to change.

Design a mountain outfit

You will need:
- card • pencil • scissors
- paints • scraps of soft, colourful materials • glue
- small beads

1 Draw outlines of the following items on the card and cut them out.

2 Paint your card clothes in bright colours. Choose some materials that would make your clothes warm and cosy. Stick them to your card clothes. How will you decorate your clothes to make them stand out against the mountain rock and snow?

Hat

Mittens

Waistcoat

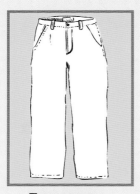
Trousers

Boots

Tourism

Mountains attract tourists who go walking and climbing in the spring and summer. Tourists also enjoy skiing, tobogganing and skating in the winter.

Skiing

Ski resorts change the natural mountain environment. Hotels, cable cars and ski lifts are built to carry skiers up the mountain to the ski slopes. Jobs are created for hotel workers and ski instructors.

Ski lifts take people to the top of a mountain slope to ski down again.

ice pick

harness

crampons

rope

This climber is using an ice pick and wearing safety equipment.

Mountain climbing

Mountain climbing needs great skill, strength, careful planning and the right equipment. Ropes and harnesses help to prevent falls, and climbing boots with steel spikes called crampons grip the ice. Ice picks help climbers to pull themselves up tough, icy slopes.

Play the mountain board game

Learn about equipment, safety, dangers, weather and making good decisions on the slopes of a mountain.

You will need:
- large sheet of card • pens and crayons • dice
- counters (or model people from self-hardening clay)

1 Copy the game shown below onto the card.

2 Take it in turns to roll the dice and move your counters across the board. Follow the instructions on the squares you land on. The first to the summit is the winner!

Now try to design a board game of your own.

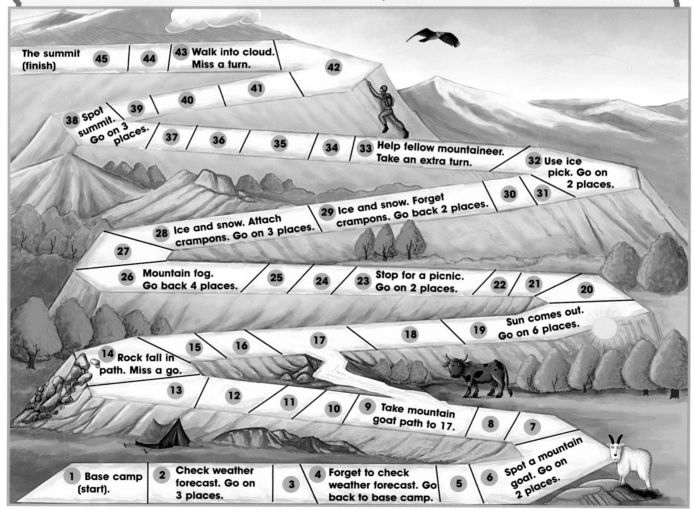

The summit (finish) — 45 — 44 — 43 Walk into cloud. Miss a turn. — 42

38 Spot summit. Go on 3 places. — 39 — 40 — 41

37 — 36 — 35 — 34 — 33 Help fellow mountaineer. Take an extra turn.

32 Use ice pick. Go on 2 places.

28 Ice and snow. Attach crampons. Go on 3 places. — 29 Ice and snow. Forget crampons. Go back 2 places. — 30 — 31

27

26 Mountain fog. Go back 4 places. — 25 — 24 — 23 Stop for a picnic. Go on 2 places. — 22 — 21 — 20

19 Sun comes out. Go on 6 places. — 18 — 17

14 Rock fall in path. Miss a go. — 15 — 16

13 — 12 — 11 — 10 — 9 Take mountain goat path to 17. — 8 — 7

1 Base camp (start). — 2 Check weather forecast. Go on 3 places. — 3 — 4 Forget to check weather forecast. Go back to base camp. — 5 — 6 Spot a mountain goat. Go on 2 places.

Caring for mountains

Mountains are wonderful places to visit. But it is important that we look after them for others to enjoy. Tourism and industry has put many mountain environments in danger.

Forests

Forests help to protect mountains. They trap and store water and prevent flooding and landslides. Timber from mountain forests is used all over the world to make paper and furniture. We can help to care for mountains by buying timber from forests that will be replanted.

Cutting down forests on the mountain slopes can cause flooding in the valleys and towns below.

Walking trails

If you visit a mountain, keep to the paths. If you stray off the path you could crush mountain plants, disturb animals or dislodge rocks and cause a rock fall. Always take litter home with you, to keep the mountain clean.

Mountains paths are designed to keep you safe and to protect the mountain.

Design a mountain poster

Think of a poster that will encourage people to care for mountains and to use them safely.

1 What do you want your poster to say?

2 Which words and pictures will get your message across?

3 Use strong, bright colours and short, catchy phrases.

Let mountain streams flow free! Take your litter home.

Keep to the path to stay safe!

Glossary

avalanche
An avalanche is a sudden rush of snow and ice down a mountain.

blizzard
A blizzard is a snowstorm with a very strong wind.

block mountain
Block mountains are formed when the Earth's plates force blocks of hard rock up or down.

broad-leaf trees
Broad-leaf trees have large leaves that fall in autumn.

camouflage
Camouflage is the way animals use their shape and colour to blend in with their surroundings.

coniferous trees
Coniferous trees have thin leaves like needles and produce cones.

crater
A crater is the hollow at the top of a volcano.

crust
The crust is the Earth's outer layer. It is made of different rocks.

erosion
Erosion is the gradual wearing away of the land by rivers and streams and by rain, wind and ice.

erupt
When a volcano erupts, hot gas and ash are thrown out into the air and lava pours down the mountain.

extinct
An extinct volcano is one that will never erupt again.

fold mountain
Fold mountains are formed when the Earth's plates push together and fold soft rocks upwards.

glacier
A glacier is a river of ice and snow that moves very slowly down the side of a mountain.

gravity

Gravity is the force that pulls objects towards the centre of the Earth.

lava

Lava is red-hot molten rock that flows from an active volcano. The molten rock is called magma when it is beneath the Earth's surface.

mammal

A mammal is a warm-blooded animal with fur or hair. Baby mammals feed on their mother's milk.

materials

Materials such as stone, wood and metal are what we use to make things.

molten rock

Molten rock is rock that has been heated to such a high temperature it has become liquid and red-hot.

peak

A mountain peak is the very highest point at the top of a mountain summit.

scree

Scree is bits of broken rock and small stones that have fallen down a mountain slope.

summit

The summit is the top of a mountain.

terrace

A terrace is a series of flat strips cut into a mountain slope to make fields for growing crops.

volcano

A volcano is a gap in the Earth's crust where hot molten rock flows through. Some volcanoes make the shape of a mountain.

weathering

Weathering is the wearing away of rock and soil by rain, ice and wind.

Index